You Can Never Go Back to the Turtle Back Inn

Jim McGarrah

ISBN: 978-81-8253-962-4

First Edition: 2022
Rs. 200/-

Rochak Publishing
HIG 45 Kaushambi Kunj, Kalindipuram
Allahabad - 211011 (U.P.) India
http://www.cyberwit.net
Tel: +(91) 9415091004
E-mail: info@cyberwit.net

Acknowledgements

Thanks to the following magazines for publishing these poems

Abramelin Magazine – "Early Morning Louisville Winter"

Avatar Review - "Drilling for Jesus" "Writer's Block" "St.Louis Cemetery"

Boomer Lit - "Waiting"

Blue Lake Review – "Chaos Theory"

Collateral – "In a Meadow Where Things Belong"

The Deadly Writers Patrol – "Lunch at the Tri Dove Cafe During the Balkans War"

December Magazine – "Christmas Day" "Every Street Goes Both Ways"

Elixir Magazine – "The Covered Bridge in Wheeling, Indiana"

Innisfree, issue 31- "Illusion, USA" "An Occasional Poem for No Occasion"

Jefferson Review – "Faustus"

Main Street Rag – "Chipped"

This book is dedicated to my friends Keith Weisheit and Ron Broadhurst, who live in my memory as true examples of good men and unnecessary casualties of the Vietnam War fifty years later. Semper Fi, my Brothers.

Contents

Prologue : News of the World

January 15, 2022, in the ancient country
of Ceylon—called Sri Lanka today—
a mother goat gave birth while stranded
in a blizzard on the side of a mountain.
A child from the nearby village carried
this goat up and over that mountain
on her tiny back. Leaning into the scream
of a tortured wind, she fought her legs
to take each step. Face blistered and numb
the child could not see, but only feel
the slow shadow of death descending
from a ceiling of low hanging clouds.
If a minute is forever to a man on fire
how long were the hours she struggled
with her assertion of worth in every life?
The family dog, frost-covered, followed
faithfully wobbling on all four legs as it
carried the baby kid home the same way.
In the "civilized" world of the U.S.A.
—state of Texas and free land of plenty—
on this same day, a mother annoyed
with her nuisance of a newly born and crying
baby beat the thing to death and then threw
its lifeless form in the nearest garbage dump.
The weather was perfect.

"Oh Mama, can this really be the end, to be stuck inside of Mobile with the Memphis blues again" – Bob Dylan

Illusion, U.S.A

Like Kudzu, a history thrives
in tiny rural towns unaware
of its desire to control an ecology
it doesn't understand. A tourist
in one of these towns sees
chifforobes, antique chairs,
newly varnished furniture,
and gilded busts of local heroes
fresh from important estate sales
crowding the sidewalks on a street
strategically called Main.
Shops full of chocolate
and old-fashioned soda fountains
outline the town square.
In this 21st century, a Farmer's Market
offers healthy changes to your diet
and a store stacked with used books makes
you think decent country folk still read.
On one of a few special days
each year, the artsy-craftsy housewives
set up tents on the courthouse lawn
to offer homemade jams, homespun quilts,
and homegrown oddities that defy definition.
There is no urban sprawl in this pastoral scene
unless you count two convenience stores
that sell gasoline and grape Slurpee's,
one McDonald's or a Pilot truck stop
just off the interstate exit a mile west
of the last Baptist church. What you won't

notice is the misery of nostalgia.
A locomotive bellows by twice a day
with empty freight cars crisscrossing Main,
its soot and stench form a cloud of shadows
that used to hold a bank, a union hall,
two schools, a library, a family doctor,
and a single room post office in paradise.

The Covered Bridge in Wheeling, Indiana

The cross beams have rotted, their skeletons spliced
with young steel. Creosote covering planks like chocolate

sticks to my boots. I trip on warped, ill-fitted boards
and stop mid-way, listening to the creek roll by.

The bridge sways slightly in the current.
My reveries are liquid, flowing into history

when hoofbeats echoed and straw rustled through the corridor.
Spider webs of sunlight filter through the roof and capture

the scarred beam where two lovers etched a heart in 1905.
I feel their breath on my neck as I trace the heart's outline.

Oil and salt, sweated from their palms long ago, leaches
into my skin and heats my blood until my own heart constricts

and connects the bank of dream to the bank memory
across a river of the past flowing beneath the bridge.

Christmas Day

I have never seen a ballet, but on any given holiday
the local schoolyard teems with pirouettes & arabesques,
an asphalt version of the great Bolshoi full of leaps, darts,
glides, and turns. It's an Assemble´ that ends in a grand jete´.

A man teaches his son to play basketball with a step left,
spin, slide right, and rush to the goal where he lays
the ball against the backboard gently. It bounces once
and falls through a hoop as the boy proclaims "Perfect."

My father taught me this exact move sixty years ago
in a damp garage on an oil-stained floor with a wicker hoop
and an out-of-round rubber ball. Those movements
have kept me dancing between pain and desire, past and present,

birth and death, alive in a place of grace with all its meanings
poise, mercy, adorn, honor—from a kind of kindness
only possible when you can teach your child to share it in a world
that has not learned how compassion becomes life and finally,
art.

Treasure

(Country Store on Kentucky Highway 79)

Inside, a Hindu dagger
and an African walking stick
next to a stack of tee shirts labeled:

Schlitz Beer
Making Ugly People Pretty for Decades

The man who ran the store confessed
he'd never met a Hindu or an African,
unless you counted old Joe Henderson
who happened to be black
and was born in a log house on the gravel road
between Harned and Leitchfield
before the end of Jim Crow.

"But, one man's junk
is another man's treasure," the storekeeper said.

Outside, the silk-soft wind ruffled
a wheat field as if it were fur on a dog's back.
The empty road went on for miles
in a wealth of silence. The deep sun bleached
a sky absent of chaos and the clutter of clouds.

In the Years of the Plague

America had me talking to myself.
Unlike prior monologues over Dylan lyrics,
Italian food, how good I might look behind
the wheel of a Porsche, whether Ted Williams
hit better than Stan Musial, is death necessary,
where do gods come from, and can trees think,
this logorrhea was born from humanity wasting
away beneath "oh beautiful for spacious skies"
atop "purple mountain majesties" and across
"amber waves of grain." Men and women
had become insane by choice. Life was
a Marquis de Sade renaissance without the sex.
And yes, I know I'm mixing metaphors
but there is no other way to explain the damage
except to say a disease prevaricated its way
into the bloodstream of my nation infecting anyone
anywhere weak-minded enough with a virus more
virulent than our most prescient pandemic, which we
named after a brand of beer, for god's sake. Think of it
like a return to the 60's when some people feared hippies
might lace the country's water supply with LSD
causing vampires, communists, space aliens, pedophiles,
Big Foot, and Fluoride to rescind white rule, except
we no longer have good drugs, clean water, or hippies.

How I Learned What's Really Important

Having lived through
twisted weather and melting ice caps, wars
and delusions of peace, plagues and poverty,
I felt confident I understood my wife's anxiety
in this 21st century of virus and viral hate
as we drove past the lake that borders our home.
The street was deserted, the oak trees were barren,

the sky hung low like a blank gray chalkboard.
Her eyes welled with tears as I offered up
a propitiatory cliché in a silly masculine way.
"Don't worry, Dear. The worst will soon be over."
"Look at the geese," she answered. Our resident goose
and gander, followed by their fuzzy hatchlings,
wandered and wobbled across the road.

I stopped the car to let them pass.
One of the chicks was missing.

Drilling for Jesus

The dentist spoke of Jesus today as she drilled a hole
in one of my molars, how she was reading Genesis
and how difficult it was to get from all that
Sodom and Gomorrah sex and blood to the same God
raising the dead and saving sinners because of love.
Numbed and nervous, I squirmed through the sound
of torture—the high-speed whir, the suck and gurgle
of a water hose, the agonizing tremolo of smooth jazz
on Sirius radio—and the stench of pain in isopropyl air.
Feeling a twinge of despair and the desire to appear
brave, I shared my pretend knowledge of theology
using a thought delivered to me a priori because I
had suffered neither recent sex nor death, forgetting
in the epiphany that my mouth was stuffed with cotton.
"Wat uff Hezeus ussent who he uss?" "What?" she said,
and the conversation left us both with an existential dread
as the truth misunderstood often will.

What if Jesus wasn't who he was.
We learn when young to hear the lie as truth
if it serves us better and we forget that things
aren't always what they seem. Forget Jesus.
I thought of Santa and how easy it was for mom
to get my compliance in the month of December.
Forget Santa Claus, Tooth Fairy, Easter Bunny, think
of my friend Bill who quit school and joined the Marines.
He wasn't a child, but he was—full of self-doubt
and a sense of duty. Like many of us in those days
that followed the days when our fathers had saved

the world, Billy believed in his own good war.
Like Billy, many of us believed as well,
and by enlisting we bought a ticket to the show.
He stumbled on a land mine with his left foot
probably. No one knows for sure.
It was one of his pieces we never found.

Chaos Theory

My German Shepard saved a chipmunk's life.

She didn't mean to.

Like a drunk driver whose car stalls
or a serial killer whose gun misfires,
it happened without altruistic intent.

The two faced off between park trail and mulberry bush
in a verdant neighborhood of vines and roots.

A tail wag, a stuttered step, the race began.
At the last instant my pet lost as her nemesis fled
beneath the earth into the tunnel of a burrowed home

while above them both an angry hawk scolded the dog
for scaring off lunch. How difficult it must have been

for the beasts involved to realize the bigger picture
and how impossible for those concerned to understand
that natural order is an illusion of natural impulse.

Context

"Life…is a tale told by an idiot, full of sound and fury, Signifying nothing." (Macbeth by Wm. Shakespeare)

Shakespeare died drinking wine
or so the legend goes

in the spring beneath a dogwood tree

Lifting one cup after another in toasts
to his friends

his hand weakened and a fever grew
strong enough to end the genius

—the one that carried
Hamlet to his grave
swept Richard from his throne
and made Romeo a romantic fool—

Some experts argue

the Bard never wrote anything of consequence
that his gift dripped from another's quill

Oxford Bacon Derby Marlowe maybe
but for whom no proof exists

I wonder if it matters
since the past is more construct
than context

History is only myth sworn to
by a shadow called memory

Isn't what's said more important
than who said it   If not

then what is a poem for

Talismans

"a people without memory are a people without a future" –
Victor Jara

If I said "Victor Jara, do you know him?" What
would you answer? He did not live in the United States,
star in movies, play sports, or win elections.

Led into a soccer stadium fifty years ago,
hands smashed because he played a guitar,
held captive for four days with no food or sleep,
his captors butchered him on the fifth for the crime
of writing songs that Chilean peasants sang.
Now, Chile bears streets named for him, plays
his songs on radios. His butchers died forgotten.

Borges wrote history down wrong. Memory doesn't
keep our talismans sacred. It's the other way around,
—bits and pieces tossed casually across a desktop,
a Zippo, a rock from a creek bed, a photo of a ballgame,
a pocket watch that doesn't work, or a few old songs
played by Victor Jara before his hands were broken
that are still sung louder than the thump of mortar shells,
the rattle of rifle fire, and the insane clatter of bones
tossed into a mass grave at a soccer stadium.

Community Affairs

Four of them sit under a tree.
After begging on street corners
in the August heat, they met for shade
to escape a sun bright enough
that even hawks hunting in the sky
above them seem blinded and confused.

Homeless,
one sat on an upturned bucket, one crouched
on each side, and the fourth perched cross-legged
on the ground facing them like the Buddhist monk
I saw facing a squad of soldiers in the streets
of Saigon many years ago.

They spoke
with broad gestures, lit cigarettes, and ignored
their own torn clothes, the dirt on their faces,
and the lean look of hunger in each other's eyes.
Smiles broke into laughter too loud for poverty.
The crowded traffic pushed and shoved on streets
around them and beyond the sanctity of their tree.
I wanted to believe these men were not poor.

Chipped

Of eight cereal bowls
stacked in the cupboard
I eat cereal from only one,
and my favorite isn't perfect.

It's chipped on the lip.
It's cracked down the side.

It's been dropped at least once by the whole family.

The blues golds greens in the pastoral scene fade
into wilted shadows of flowers and trees.

I feed myself from this bowl in secret so my wife
won't keep telling me to throw it away.
It's broken, which is not the same as useless.

Portrait in Shades of Blues

My father had no desire to suffer
needlessly. He was no martyr—
a reluctant war hero maybe. He denied
that label as well. Dad gambled, cursed,
attended church, gave money to charities,
did business with everyone in the county
as an honest and helpful man who made
no enemies that didn't deserve to be.
A white man in the Eisenhower era,
he watched Fred Astaire movies
at the theater and played Bing Crosby
on a jukebox at our small-town VFW.
My father showed his family love as he
was taught and understood love should
be shown, with grace, patience, and duty.
But when his world became a blue place
full of memories, he bought cheap whiskey,
retreating to a small room in our large home
with a stack of records, a paper cup, and a bag
full of ice. There he sat with buried friends,
numbed by a war he had fought and memories
he never asked for. He wailed through
each record. The songs seeped between
a narrow crack in the French doors, rolled
along the hallway and into my bedroom
late at night. I listened to his off-key cry
in melodies carried perfectly nowhere
but in his primal mind. His choir
had magical names—Blind Willie,

John Lee Hooker, Howlin' Wolf, Son House,
Ray Charles, Robert Johnson, Furry Lewis.
In strange harmonies, they all sang sad words
about crossroads and killing floors and perils
of love with a feeling that my father knew
the war had taken and in a voice he wanted back.

Back at the Turtle Back Inn

I have no memory of the first time I met
my father's friend Fats Domino years ago
when my father was alive. I know they shot
craps together, often rolling the dice in Vegas
or some back street alley behind a dive bar
till both had emptied their pockets. Those tales
were shared as legends at each family summit.
They were bad gamblers and that made them good
friends. Dad always said, "Water seeks its own level."

Here's the thing—I did meet the great singer
fifty years ago on some sawdust and blood dance floor
outside Cincinnati, but when I think of those young days
it's only of Cathie, her body trembling with the touch
of his piano and her cheeks flushed crimson with wine,
the flame that rose in her eyes if you happened

to beat her at a game of 8 ball, the hint of self-doubt
in her oblique smile, the way she wore her jeans
and the way she took them off, and the music
the air made when she danced. How easily I forgot Fats
that night he pounded a piano till his fingers bled
and the crowd on the dance floor swayed

with the rise and fall of every note. Maybe it's love,
which is always present tense, not future or past.
Maybe it's the mercy of memory, which gives us
small moments so we don't miss the hours time steals.
I'd like to believe that Fats would take no offense
at my forgetfulness, especially if he had known Cathie.

Leda

She glides over an untilled field
as if it were a smooth lake toward you.
Her perfectly pale neck rises from a silk shirt
that shrouds the flaws exposed by wakening
as the day begins to bare her.

As she raises a wrist to your cheek,
skin as thin as gauze kisses your mouth
and her veins burn like blue flame
against your lips. Above you both

a swan flies into the horizon,
a small star falling out of sight.

Waiting

(for Keith)

In a room where I hoped to never be,
jigsaw puzzles unfinished on tabletops
remind me that everything has limits.
Magazines of good advice and full
of perfect lives no one ever lives
are stacked neatly in wooden racks.
I am surrounded by safe earth tones.
Taupe is popular in these places.
Landscape prints of meadows
for picnics or the loss of virginity
adorn the walls, along with framed
photos of founders and philanthropists.
I can find brochures of any disease
to ignore the one I have.
A vase of cut roses stands on a table
centered around a few empty chairs.
They are the most beautiful of flowers
right before they die.

Progress

It must have been '71, or maybe '72.
You sat on a bar stool in some dive bar
with sawdust and peanut shells spread
across the floor in a blanket of fake nostalgia.
It was Middletown, New York.
Bob Dylan and The Band wrote music
nearby, and a woman you wanted to love
forever, but couldn't, didn't know you yet.
You hoped the mescaline never wore off
and wished the warm beer would taste better.
He sat down next to you, this vacant-eyed guy,
and asked where to buy a decent burger.
You were young and believing in America
answered McDonald's. "What's that?" he said,
confessing he spent the last thirty years in prison.
You spoke of all our progress—Jonas Salk
wiped out polio, a Catholic got elected president,
a brave woman name Rosa refused to give up
her seat on the bus, music got political, a war
was almost over, fast food, color TV, cassette tapes,
LSD, and the rise of technology—skipping politely
over the murder and misery shared in those events.

Early Morning Louisville Winter

A man in a grey overcoat that matches the sky leers at his image
in the glass of a deserted service station, leans into the wind,
and totters towards a liquor store next door. Ice crystals crunch

on the pavement like eggshells with each lilted step. A child jogs
past the Lutheran church across the street, his stocking cap
pulled low in adolescent defiance of the cold clawing at his face.

It's a life-size Hopper painting framed in bleak and black.
A flock of grackles spirals downward, a frantic funnel unrolling
as a vast feathered carpet over the empty park where I sit

and wait for Number 19, the bus that will carry me across town.
Rays from a burnished-rust sun begin to tease the clouds. Soot
and smoke spits from the chimneys of the whiskey distilleries.

A Midwest misery of early delivery trucks scatters over streets.
Winter is always downcast for me. I'm at an age when the past
is mostly imagined and the future more hope than expectation.

A few bodies march along sidewalks and, like Sisyphus, roll
their lives uphill to work. Some will climb again tomorrow
forced by morphic resonance, others with a mindful resignation.

I feel alone, isolated in the swirls of grime, like litter
being covered by flakes of pristine snow, and lost behind
a gauzy upswept fog in the gusts blowing over steel and brick.

To Sweep the Soot Away

When his marriage ended
my brother became a chimney sweep.

A filthy job, I thought it must fulfill
an urgent economic need—bills to pay,

two boys to support, an ex-wife.
Why else would any person

wait for the stilled wind to still
the dust and dirt and dead feathers

from the brick funnels
atop those slick and steepled roofs?

"Unnoticed and with a view over streets
full of well-lit homes," he told me

was how he liked to visit
happiness, how it rose

in the sweet smell of pine smoke
and how, breathing in the ashes

from each family around the fire, he could
wish for a life his own life had denied.

Cruising in the Quarantine in 2021

Purple wisteria explodes between stop signs
along Mill Ridge Avenue. Like a Cezanne,
the foreground of our diseased spring rises
in contrast to the background—the empty park,
houses teeming with unemployed tenants,
the vacant stores, the trees hovering
between green and brown.

In the past, I cruised town this same way,
quarantined by youth and boredom
rather than the fear of death. In those days
my body purred with the same
deep-throated growl as the dual exhausts
on my cherry-red '57 Chevy.
Man, I loved that car.
It poured me into the dark well
of those pure spring nights, and I ripped
through all four gears laying rubber
between the pale-yellow light of streetlamps.
In high school the best way to look hip
was to be moving away from something.
Now, I'm struck in a time loop where a present
of faded color and empty streets multiply
contagious fears exponentially and every day.

The Price of Salvation

I taught *The Glass Menagerie* for one semester
in an abandoned lab on a sugar cane farm.
The students came from Haiti to find
a better way of life.

They spoke a patois stewed from French
and English while rats, fat on sugarcane stalks,
climbed the walls like Sherpa guides as I explained
why Laura collected glass unicorns in a tiny zoo
to students who had never seen a zoo.

Unwashed and underfed, some without parents,
and some who supported parents by working
in cane fields before, during, and after school,
they struggled to understand Laura's despair
with empty bellies, and the hollow stares
of beasts more dead than alive.

In the Sunset a Symphony of Sad Gold

In a solar storm
the earth hums an eerie sound
like an out-of-tune violin.
Pretend sunlight is a bow,
magnetic fields are strings.

Listen.

Experts have logged the song.
It's the same one that plays
in our primal brain each day
at sunset, roils our stomachs
till a slight shiver of ineluctable
welcome for the gloaming shadows
hints that night, like death, spawns
the exquisite horror of darkness.

Point of Reference

1.

For a child it's a mother's breast.
For mother, the rough suck of her child.
For absence it's desire.
For desire, pain.

2.

She suffered months of morning sickness,
a swelled belly, and a roller coaster ride
of hormonal ups and downs. Her menses
stopped, and her breast ached so bad
she couldn't button a soft cotton blouse.
Her womb grew bigger week after week.

3.

My aunt, pregnant by a desire
no man could comprehend
gave birth to air.

Varnished

His ex-wife refinished—desks
rocking chairs, end tables,
coffee tables, nightstands,
and chifforobes—anything
with rough edges and scars
that could be smoothed
by grinding with fine sandpaper,
planing flaws from existence,
and staining the blanched wood
a brunet color.

Transubstantiated varnish
became the blood of Jesus
and a paint brush the mode
of transformation.
The basement in their home
housed her altar,
and she took him there hoping
to refurbish him by sharing
her passion.

It might have worked
had he been less damaged
by the wear and hard use
of their marriage.

The Shit Wars

My last year in high school
pigeons attacked the clock tower
atop the county courthouse.
Hundreds roosted in cracks and crevices
along the gutters and on the roof.
Pigeon shit painted the town square.
The flying grey rats shat on lawyers,
the old circuit judge, the county clerk
and the beehive hairdos of her all-female
staff, even the credit criminals
as they snuck into a court for bad debts.
These winged demons held no regard
for status or beauty. They dive-bombed
Cadillac's and Chevy's alike. They defaced
park benches and Civil War statues.

Enough was enough. The mayor phoned
the county game warden who arrived
one morning with six shotguns
loaded with double ought bird shot
and a coffee thermos full of bourbon.
We skipped class to watch the carnage
through the plate-glass window
of the Palace Pool Hall across the street.

For three hours it rained feathers and blood.
The sky filled with blue smoke.
The air stank of cordite and bird entrails.
Gunfire rattled shop windows

and shopkeepers carped like scalded dogs.
Pigeon parts were carted off sidewalks
by a gang of feral cats.
My friends, filled with bloodlust,
cheered as the body count rose.
I was ambivalent regarding violence
but did not want to be embarrassed
by a less than manly attitude.
I cheered the loudest of them all.

Letting Go

Watch the ground beneath an oak tree
as frost settles on the tree's limbs
and across its variegated leaves.

An Occasional Poem for No Occasion

Honeysuckle rises
in a spring perfume of gasoline
from a neighbor's leaky lawnmower
and onions boiling with garlic
in the Nigerian stew next door.

It's a typical May day. The sun shines.
Two deer graze near the woods across
Highway 29. My dog trees a squirrel.
Somewhere someone is dying.
At 9AM my daughter bought a new car.

My son drove his old one to work.
A slight ripple of wind ruffles
the sea of dandelions near Walmart
and a siren screams in the distance. Why
is the world working so hard to implode?

In a copse of pine trees near a parking lot
crows glisten as they glean the ground
around a single metal trash bin adding
mystery to a theme of urban isolation
that would make Edward Hopper proud.

No one can define love anymore.
We have dulled the senses that create
the word. But there is no evil in my heart
this morning, and I'm as close to being
born after being born as anyone ever gets.

Boomers

1.

Born at the end of a world war opera,
we were as Parsifal, the seed
of a Wagnerian god and raised to be
kings in search of a holy grail.
The bag of gold our fathers fought
for us to carry, so weighted by the sins
we have caused in filling it, has begun
to tip us over the edge of our own abyss.

2.

Who will be left to forgive us
when the thrum of our armies falls
silent and the hard tears of the wind
rusts our death machines, when
the disappeared have re-appeared
in upturned shallow graves, in caves
filled with bleached bones, and beneath
the deserts that once grew towns
with names sounding like flowers?

3.

Macaroni and cheese,
a Cadillac and Johnny Walker Blue,
72 degrees and a gentle breeze.
A different soul mate every night

—a mansion in a meadow
a mansion on a mountain
a mansion on the beach
good health and health insurance

peace in our homes
one billion dollars tax free
Jesus and Dow Jones
J.P. Morgan
A wine cellar—

and all etcetera's
we could possibly inherit.
The irony of having is
that it never becomes enough.

4.

When we reached puberty.
we swore our allegiance
in church to the dead body
of our savior while dreaming
of the girls around us in the pews.

Baptized, we felt no remorse over
the Jungian duality of man and drank
the communion wine for its effect.

Our fathers taught us to abstain
from sex and gin on Easter,
and we gave our mothers hope
their sons might learn the value
of those Eisenhower illusions
that made their loneliness worthwhile.

5.

We learned women came from
a woman named Eve, and Eve
was made from one rib of a guy
named Adam. No one ever asked
why men weren't missing a rib.

6.

We grew into the big dogs
stretched out on the warm wood
of our master's deck.

Now, we raise a lazy paw
to scratch an imaginary flea,
yawn, fart, roll over, and return to our nap.

Spreading the Word

The Bible tells the story of a man named Jesus
who cast demons out from two other men
and into a herd of swine. The pigs, full
of evil, threw themselves off a nearby cliff
and perished. That is a parable. But this is true:
If a man, ignorant of pigs and the sounds
they make, listening to the squeals and seeking
comfort in the noise of many, stumbles into their pen,
they will devour him including the bones
without thought and with no remorse by the herd.

Theseus Paradox

You can feel seasons begin
to change even in southern Georgia.
Ever had a tick drop on the back
of your neck and fade into your hair
before you catch it? Then,
you know what I mean.
The sun still blinds you and burns
green grass brown in patches.
The days wear on, but not as hot.
The dog's naps grow shorter
after lunch, and the flies slow down
drugged by the lethargy of dying.
A breeze makes you shiver
and a few leaves fall without reason.
Maybe a paradox comes to mind,
an irony applied to you by virtue
of biology and wishful thinking.
What nature will sluff off in the next
few weeks of autumn has not died.
Your world is being replaced, but not.
What returns in the spring is the same,
but different. The same flowers
bloom with new petals, trees regain
green leaves, worms till the dead soil
and the same lawn needs mowing.
Think of an old philosopher's question,
"If you step in the same river twice
is it really the same river?"
Heraclitus will say yes,
Plutarch will say no.
What if both are right?

"Seeking what is true is not seeking what is desirable."
- Albert Camus

When a Truth has No Reason to Be True

(For John and Brittany)

A kind man goes for lunch at a small café in upstate New York.
Before you ask, "is this true?" This is true, not *a priori*
in a mystical sense, or metaphorically in an analogous sense
because it's impossible to know when you walk a street
for the last time, but in the sense that it happened.

After lunch, the man stands beside his daughter—her hand
on his shoulder—in a parking lot full of cars, trees, and gravel.
They speak of nothing important as a limousine pieced together
from salvaged scraps, brakes failing, a hunk of junkyard junk
ordered off the road months before by State Police, blasts
through a stop sign like Slothrop's rocket in *Gravity's Rainbow*
and carries eighteen passengers down a hill above that café.

As you might expect, every passenger dies when it hits the tree.

It's a damn wreck of a car having a car wreck.

But this man, speaking nothing important to his daughter
is caught alone in a wave of metal, swept away and crushed.

Somewhere the ghost of Albert Camus might be laughing,
except this story is true—remember?—and ghosts don't laugh.

That's absurd.

The 2nd Amendment as Taught in School

The Ohio river flows west
as I drive east in a thunderstorm.

It's the middle of America
during another planting season.

As the water roils unfettered
above flood stage

and scoops topsoil from the fertile land
between highway and levee

the current churns the young earth into cold
dark lava that washes all the seeds away.

Seeing David at the Uffizi in Florence, Italy

The calm in the center of a single moment
is that instant when an origin arrives.
The future spins into life from this nucleus.

There is a thrill as to what it might do,
as to where it might go—what to grasp,
what has slipped away, what to reach for—

Sometimes it swirls into a vanishing point,
abandons, strands without hope.
How many times did Michelangelo

walk around that block of marble before
David was born? How many times did he stumble
before finding a silence that changed the future of art?

Chagall's "The Poet Reclining"

(Painted During WWI in 1915)

The barn is fenced by fir trees, one pig
in the sty, a dappled horse tethered and grazing nearby.

In the foreground of the canvas a slim man lies with his head
on a folded beige jacket, hands clasped across his chest
in funereal pose, a crumpled hat tossed behind him casually.

From the expressionless face narrow slits replace eyes
that could be closed or merely squinting in an impotent attempt

to not notice what, as a poet, he must discern estranged
from the painter's pastoral ideal—a war being fought
around the edges of Chagall's canvas. His illusory calm

disappears, betrayed by the ashen pallor on his face
and just beyond the vanishing point, a ravaged violet sky.

Breakfast in 4/4 time

In the middle of sizzle & splash,
a waiter of dubious sanity adds
to xylophonic scales played
by sandals, sneakers, and chairs

sliding across the tiled floor.
Dressed like a cabaret emcee
in 1930's Germany, he scoots
between tables and whistles

tunes out of tune under
the hum of bearings in a ceiling fan.
Caught in counterpoint
between doom and day

as laughter and tickling spoons
inside of coffee cups join the crescendo.
The sounds merge with his rhythm
like Tchaikovsky's 6th symphony

and the movement
of a conductor's baton,
leaving him to dance in limbo
between loneliness and the crowd.

Dog Days

1

—Scouring old notebooks
Hiking in the forest
Watching a river flow
Driving through crowded streets
Brushing teeth
Reading novels with tired plots
Drinking bad coffee
Drinking cheap gin
Conversing with the mailman
Sweating Sweating Sweating
Doing pushups
Baking brownies—

2

No one wills the muse.
Maybe a limerick will emerge
during happy hour if you have a pen
and a cocktail napkin and if the waitress
has left you alone to suffer the indignity
of being alone, and if you're willing
to struggle, but not the poem.
Poetry appears like a pimple,
like love or a tumor. It trespasses
on your sanity, and yet you welcome
the anxiety as a dog welcomes a breeze
in the last days of indolent August.

The Quest

A child sprints around
the supermarket aisle
following his shadow

oblivious to his mother's
stern cries to stop the madness

Driven
by a force he doesn't understand
a need no parent can control
the child won't quit until

he catches
the darkness inside the shadow
and it satisfies his hunger

Getting a Haircut

1. Hometown, Indiana

Outside the window
against a gray shroud of sky
starlings by the hundreds roost
like notes in a sheet music scale
along the high electric wires.

The barber laments firing
his latest assistant as shears
run a ruin around
your nearly naked ears.
In his boredom he will never know

how much a local trim,
the familiar scent of bay rum,
a warm wet towel across
the back of your bent neck,
and the familiar tedium comforts you.

2. On the Road

Four dead deer adorn the walls
of Johnny's Barbershop surrounded
by a school of stuffed fish,
a calendar for the auto parts store
that features a bikinied babe
photo'd with a set of sparkplugs,
two bottles of talc, a jar of combs,
and the trill of an overworked
air conditioner. The tepid air hangs
low with a scent of tonsured men
laughing as the bad jokes swim
upstream against subject matter
between Mohammed, slavery,
and the width of a vagina.

One man used to cut
his own hair but says he lost
interest in abstract sculpture.

You wanted a haircut on your drive
from home in Indiana southward,
but you wonder why you chose
Georgia, a place with an uneasy twitch
like the skin on the neck of a horse
tickled by the legs of a fly.

3. Parris Island

On the cool tile floor
hair piles high like haystacks
burned autumnal from yellow
into red, brown, and black
by a late summer sun.
You wait in a long line
out the screen door
with young men who are alive
and some who soon are not,
who began the day as one of many
sheared bald by the wild rattle
of metal clippers held to even
strokes by machine-like barbers
until you all become many of one.

Love Sonnet of Naphthenic and Palmitiz

When their entwined bodies
fell from far above the clouds
the Romeo and Juliet of fire
brought death with their desire,
a flame that outshone the sun
and reduced a verdant land
to powdered gray ash.
Formed from salts and esters
by the gods of oil and sand
their passion sucked the breath
from every life within their reach.
Without regard for innocence
or evil, they brought the earth ruin
so their blighted love might reign.

The Coconut Monk

Ong Dao Dua lived on Sam Mountain
and ate nothing but coconuts as the war
raged around him in the Mekong Delta.
Legend has it he never laid down to sleep
during the carnage, praying upright
to all available gods in every religion
for an end to violence as he looked out
over the banyan trees, toucans, rock apes
and orchids on a peaceful Phoenix Island
not far from Saigon. No bombs or bullets
ever struck his home and what he missed
in life was never there to begin with.

Manifest Destiny

In platoon formation every morning
Lee Jara marched beside me on the base
at Little Creek waiting out our discharge
after fighting a war for a cause that, by then,
escaped me and I'm not sure Lee ever knew.
He was a friend, Navaho, reservation-raised,
who granted me absolution for being white.
I didn't understand his kindness in my youth.
We had invaded Vietnam and dispatched
its people with the same righteous indignation
my ancestors displayed destroying Lee's.

I'm seventy now and I have no hope
that Lee's still alive. There are very few
old braves on reservations anymore. I hope
they buried him like the warrior he was
beside the bones of his ancestors sacrificed by mine.
Lee never spoke of cultural guilt, and I laughed
at his "injun" jokes. We accepted our savage
and flawed humanity as brothers from different worlds.

Coming Home

Almost midnight and the first day of January.
You're stuck inside of Jackson, Tennessee, halfway
between the blues of Memphis and the twang
of Nashville on a road that leads away from death.
The bus stops in front of the blue Greyhound station.
It's only you and the driver. He wishes you luck,
says "thank you for your service, Marine,"
and unseals the door discharging you into
the dark New Year.

Neon lights flash overhead. The hiss and crackle
of dying bugs flush against the hot bulbs drive
you into the cavernous terminal where you
breathe in air bereft with vomit and muscatel,
where lifeless shadows from the high ceiling lights
gouge at the emptiness that used to be your soul.
Bells echo from some far-off corner waking
the taste of ashes and a tremble in your dull thoughts.
A young man in a pink jumpsuit sprinkled with sequins
grinds his narrow hips into a solitary pinball machine.

Your uniform terrifies the pinball player.
He seems unsure of your intentions and stares at you
with a glazed vacancy reflected in his eyes.
He steps from the flashing pinball machine as if space
might save him from some impending doom. He doesn't
understand what real fear can be or from where it comes.
Jealous of his innocence, you respond with the words
"Happy New Year." And, walk away into the world alone.

Agent Orange

Years ago, I sat back lit
and entranced by black light beneath
posters of Jimi and Janis. Fried
on speed in a dorm room
paid for by the G.I. Bill, I waited
for the great American novel to filter
through a Dexedrine haze
so I could publish my way to fame.

America has always had a chemical formula for success.

The year before I wrote this first chapter
was fogged with tear gas, dazed by the perfume
of napalm and doused with Agent Orange.

What's a few tabs of Dexedrine to a man
whose body has been drowned in the wake
of all that hazardous waste?

Sacrifice and hunger
fire and chaos
words.

I believed that nonsense in those
speed-fueled nights pretending
those words were real and not a bruise
on my soul that would never heal.
Little did I know that cells
still unformed and unnamed

had begun their mutation. Knowledge
would not have saved me anyway.

Tropes came fast
as if I pulled on the threads of war
and the world unraveled—
Toucans and banyans, bamboo and vipers,
elephants and tigers, a few fig trees
with rhesus monkeys resting on limbs,
the dense beauty of the coffee farms steaming
after a Monsoon rain, the scent of breakfast pho
rising into a diamond white sky and oh my god
the orchids the orchids—disappearing as the planes
dusted the white mist like burning snow across
the jungle where my squad walked patrols,
where mama-sans pregnant with a generation
of dying babies tended the poisoned rice paddies.

Tacitus knew Dioxin as a Roman god
two thousand years before Monsanto
stole his history to strip my jungle bare.

"ubi solitudinem faciunt, pacem appellant"
Where they make a desert, they call it peace.

Saint Louis Cemetery # 1

In New Orleans
the dead don't get buried.
They sleep above ground like the rest of us
in their crypts of white stone guarded
by gargoyles and frozen angels.

We are told
by urban planners that this must be

because the sea rises
above the soil
and floods every grave.

Really, the dead prefer
the company of the living

—the tourists and hucksters
the waiters and strippers
the gangsters and addicts
the cashiers and clerks
the car dealers and pimps—

who prey upon their neighbors
and are preyed upon by them.

The dead
prefer beignets and blues and the rattle of rain
to the silence of dirt and the company of worms.

It has to do
with dismembered memories

—bones and buttons
ashes and dust
a bag full of shadows—

Various Stages of Resurrection

1.

Every Easter
as if my childhood sweetened fantasies
were raised from the ashes of mom's
stern counsel—no snacks before meals,
no cereal with the first name Frosted,
no sugar in or on anything remotely edible.
These commands, among a host
of other tortuous rules designed to limit
free will, got overruled by the glory
of my Father who, suffering from gin guilt
and hungover, bribed me into
a Sunday morning pre-church silence
with chocolate donuts formed in the shape
of bunny rabbits by the local baker.

2.

I reached an age of conformation
and swore allegiance to the dead
body of a savior while dreaming
more of a girl named Denise sitting
in the pew on my right and less of candy.
I felt some remorse over this newly found
Jungian duality of man and drank
communion wine to forget, which those days
was Welch's Grape juice. You couldn't
pray for salvation with liquor on your lips

in our Protestant world. Even dad abstained
on Easter morning to give my mother hope.

3.

Choked with the scent of funereal lilies
and buried in a pool of chlorinated water
I arose one Easter not quite cleansed
of sugar highs and sexual fantasies
shrouded in a false cloak of magic babble
that Jesus lived in me as the man
I was supposed to be, instead of the boy
I was who couldn't sleep that night,
terrified of a horrible death
by the age of thirty-three.

It's All History to Me

That sage advice from fast food companies and the sellers
of self-help books urging us all to "live in the moment"
or "live in the present" or "live in the now" and not dwell
upon the past where all our nasty demons and ex-lovers live
sounds profound, as if a mystic may have meditated years
in a dank cave just to discover that each second of his life
passed like the last, or a hipster stumbled on *carpe diem*
in an old Latin text he carried to look cool at Starbuck's.
It's as if we have forgotten how time really works.
Time moves as a river, baseball game, stream of piss,
bullets fired in hundreds of different wars, all things born.

My poor brain, and I suspect yours,
senses nothing for the first one-thirtieth of one second
as it is occurring, and that's if you're sober.
Everything that I'm aware of has happened in the past.
It's true, you can't make this shit up. I'm doomed
to watch a movie of my entire life instead of living it.
Think of the effect on scientists who hope to make a new find
or a lover who has only a vague memory of a shared
orgasm. I can't even shoot myself if this knowledge
causes me an existential type of dread. I will be dead already.

The Fighter Pilot's Hobby

(In Fond Memory of Marvis Manning)

He came home from WWII as a ghost.
Declared dead by the Defense Department,
he had lain for years back broken, wasting away
in a Nazi prison camp with nothing to keep him

sane but faces on the stamps stored in his album
back home. He repasted each face daily on pages
in his struggling mind. The British Penny Black
was a favorite as the Queen's image bore

a shadowed profile to that of his wife.
He slept in exotic countries from Madagascar
to the Cayman Islands, Bahrain to Spain, China
to Turkey, and back. "I loved New Zealand's Kiwi bird,"

he told his family when he came home in 1945.
What he sought those next few years was to focus
on the loudness of the silence among his stamps,
a terrible stillness magnified by the slight crinkle

of a turning pagc in his small office.
What he loved was to imagine lands not on fire,
rivers free from blood, and an album of more
than nightmares in the light of every day.

Faustus

None of us knows everything
we don't know.
Did my life begin during a quickie
in the back seat of a '47 Ford
when the condom broke
or twenty years later
when a grenade killed the man
beside me, and I didn't get a scratch?

The moon shines
never knowing light of its own.
Beethoven never heard
the music of the Ninth Symphony.
Who is Satan, really?
Where do all the gods take
their summer vacations?
Why does the duckbilled platypus exist?

Some answers, like pi, raise questions
forever without an answer.
A woman in Taiwan was found
to have four bees under her eyelids
feeding off her tears.
No one, not even the woman herself,
knows which tears nourished the bees more,
those of joy or those of sorrow.

What Happens if You Never Stop

Drive far enough west at dusk and you outrun
darkness proving time is unnatural,
a Coriolis effect to fight chaos,
the way the planet curves to make you
trust you need somewhere to get to
like a retirement party or a third martini.
This marvel pelts you first in the eastern
part of Kansas with a rain of clichés—majestic,
sprawling, endless, scenic, uncluttered,
and grand—all hyperbole for flat.
Keep driving. Light will go on forever.
The sky opens and scoops the land up whole.
Where you are it is day, where you were
it remains the night before.
If you could drive far enough
would darkness disappear?

Being Human

One of life's hard lessons
is finding out I am not necessary,
a fact that transcends family,
city, state, country, or liquor store.
I wallow without
purpose in the grand scheme
of Nature and remain
excessive, unneeded, gratuitous.

Trees and bees would argue I am
detrimental to the daily skills required
for every instinctive process from sex
through photosynthesis and arrogant
in my own ignorance of that fact.
Dying reminds me too late of my own
unimportance.

In a Small Woods Near Our Home

The dog barks at a scent in the gloaming
and a cow that must have wandered
into the drunken sight of a hunter forms
a corpse beneath a copse of oaks.

Crows, startled by motion, lift off
the leafless limbs, their blackness outlined
on the Wagnerian sheet music of a grey sky.

They are free of all gravity except the fear
of a lean winter that may soon follow autumn.

The dog and I greet two does making a home
with their fawns around a wall of wisteria
and red buckeye as they dance along
the ravine between us. By the soft whistle

through the tops of a few scattered pines
I am reminded of how the wind plays a music
too often unheard. A melody without words,

without time, rises above the noise of being
human and is joined by a chorus of distant thunder.

In a Meadow Where Things Belong

On the small patch of barren dirt
seeded with grass refusing to grow,
a neon green tennis ball sprouts.

I am miles from any tennis court
in a meadow preserved for birds,
squirrels, chipmunks, and worms,

which proves to me that ironic
juxtaposition is a flaw in human
behavior and not the quirk

of a chaotic universe. Reflections
such as this remind me of Rick
our Navy corpsman in combat.

He was a gentle man who cured
sick children with chocolate bars
and patched the wounded as we bled.

One day Rick arrived where he didn't
belong in a meadow reserved for dying
not healing. Not wanting to upset

the balance of nature, he placed a rifle
beneath his own chin and compressed
the trigger softly as if it might break.

My Father's Mother

Grandma plowed
perfect rows
behind the family mule,
wrung an unsuspecting
chicken's neck
in the blink of an eye,
baked a cherry pie,
and cut a chord of firewood
as grandpa ate breakfast,
or so my father said.

She taught
us grandkids manners
and made the best fudge
in Gibson County.

Except for the Bible
Grandma never read much
and believed mostly what
the crows sang.
She never learned
to drive a car.

How do you know
what memories
to keep or let go
the older you grow?

Mostly, I remember her shoes

called Clodhoppers—square-toed
uneven at the heels from pacing
the floor with my baby sister
during episodes of colic
and slit between sole and toe
to ease the pain of bunions.
Those shoes were sturdy
in order to steady a wild boy,
not stylish but perfect
for the labors she loved.

The Golden Years

A single misstep on a flight of stairs,
the stumble over a simple word or a stutter
in a guffaw while no one else is laughing,
the scent of wood ash or rotting lilies in a room,
a touch too late on the brake at a busy intersection
or the glazed gaze staring through the reflection
in the mirror. Maybe you left the oven on after lunch.

Old age appears as the reign of tears at the end of an old movie
when the dog dies, rain that drums on a tin roof through
a bright gauze of fog & sun, the taste of a ripe peach,
or the last few notes of an old song replayed on the radio.

It's a new hip or a knee or attending a school reunion
minus a few classmates from the last one, a dread
that certain things can no longer be done, like climbing
Mount Everest or buttoning your favorite shirt.
Dreams become confused for memories,
and those memories seem as real as dreams.

To the Young French Women
On the Bayou Boat Tour

You are life
leaning on the brass rail
and laughing at the sunlight
as it ignites
the black water.

You are orchids,
flowers of an ancient forest,
both elegant and wild,
blooming among the beasts
in this swamp

—alligators, snowy egrets,
snakes that curl around
the cypress limbs, panthers,
and ospreys that are mounted
like pearls on cork oak trees—

What blossoms from your delight
sows the kernel that keeps
the rest of us alive.

Lunch at Tri Dove Cafe During the Balkan Wars

You have traveled a coastal road to Piran
and found yourself hungry like the sea gulls
pouting around a barren Adriatic surf.
Old men mend nets on the bows of boats,
a rainbow of canvas sails ripples above them.
The harbor hums a lullaby in the warm breeze.

One bow-tied waiter serves squid with Lasko beer,
the scent of salt air churns beside the sea wall.
Over the sidewalk a boy skates, his legs lift
and fall piston-like in time to metal wheels
along the pavement and clatter of trailing children.
He is a pied piper of laughter and tourist chatter.

Hucksters sell souvenirs from three-sided booths
lined along the quay. Look across the bay.
You can see Croatia from here in Slovenia through
the crystalline curtain of sunlight shimmering over
the dead Adriatic Sea. Smoke from burned towns leaks
into white clouds above the thump of mortar shells.

The rattle of rifle fire reminds the dead there why
being dead is hard work. They must convince the living
at a quiet lunch to digest the grief with the taste of tiramisu.

Veterans Administration Sonnet of Certifiability

Being a veteran injured in some war
gets my widow two thousand dollars
toward funereal expenses provided
she can prove that I died of a disease
directly related to said war such as
bullet placement or Agent Orange.
Syphilis or the clap don't count.

My passing must be proven to the VA
specifically. But only if a bureau within
that bureau receives a form notarized proving
my demise uncontaminated with normal mortality.
Otherwise, she gets two hundred and fifty
as my particular dying is deemed improperly fatal.

The Island on an Island

(Washington Park, in Greenwich Village, Circa 1969)

Before my Icarus soul fell
from its flight of urban grace,
I soared along city streets
hand in hand with a woman I loved.

Before Ginsberg and Burrows woke
to scour Mott Street in search of Benzedrine
to speed up their morning coffee,
she and I drank Genesee on Sundays

at Googie's Bar, convinced by drunks
still drinking from the night before
that stale beer and urine was a perfume
worn inside the smoky room by loneliness.

Along MacDougal Street foul exhaust
from diesel engines fouled the air,
In the Park a sweeter fuel of hemp
burned with jasmine and sweat

as fugitives from upstate suburbs
nested at the feet of the latest Dylan clone,
and the music fused them from different facets
into the same rough diamond of lost and bored youth.

Time wore on the faces of the old Jews—refugees
from World War II and a blown up, burned down

Europe— lining the sidewalks nervously
playing chess on the chessboards that dotted

the Park's corners like cement toadstools. The men
cursed in their native tongues when they missed
a move or maybe remembered a family buried deep
beneath the camps that were their former homes.

Unmasked around the old and young to a lustful sun
and the misery of night's exhausted shadows,
a steel and glass city rose from this swirling sea
where she and I moored beneath the salmon-colored sky.

My Favorite Time

arrives with winter
right before dawn
when the wind

tosses frozen dew across empty streets
and it crackles like burning cinders
beneath my feet
when the first

lamps bloom in rows of houses
and children rise from bed
to meet the day with a hunger
that heats the cold air

My favorite time
arrives right before sunrise

as gray light

carries away the chaos of my dreams
from their silent chorus in my mind
and leaves me alone for an instant
in the sanctuary of a new day

I can do anything
in my favorite time

before the sun

sculpts my shadow in its own way

"I Won't Dance, Don't Ask Me"

(From the movie Roberta, starring Fred Astaire, 1935)

A rage of rhythm
A dervish of delight

You can hear the flow if you listen

a whirlpool of cartilage ligament veins arteries spinning
around in a wild ocean of muscle and bone struggling
to erupt into the musical sky

You can see the thoughts if you look

inside the brain flashing random impulses
electricity gone crazy buzzing and redirected
on each drumbeat

patterns only possible by a genius in motion
the davening of a god on celluloid

You can almost bear the joy

Do you feel it

Celluloid Suggestions

Just once, I wish James Bond
took out the trash literally.
Make it one of those trash bags
that break from the weight of a Kleenex
spilling hideous streams of eggshells,
coffee grounds, rotten banana peels,
& tampons over his fancy Italian loafers.

What if Jason Bourne forgot
to bring home a gallon of milk
as demanded by his lover
of a nonspecific gender as required
by current correctness in social circles,
after an evening of random slaughter
and got his ass kicked for his forgetfulness.

Maybe Captain Kirk could take a tab
of LSD in lieu of a Vulcan mind-meld,
flipping out at Scotty's accent,
and throw himself out of a space lock
as he shouts, "look at the pretty points
on Ohura's rainbow-colored chest."
Spock might even laugh.

Don't forget Mary Poppins,
that bitch is just too happy.
Or the Von Trapp family, which deserved
a punishment equal to sitting through

A Sound of Music every year at Easter
after a double-featured nightmare
of *The Ten Commandments* and *King of Kings.*

How much better would *A Wonderful Life* be
with Freddy Kruger as protagonist or *Harry Potter,*
all four thousand and fifty-seven episodes,
if Hermione had grown up to be a stripper.
Why can't Hollywood find more actors of color
so Samuel L. Jackson and Morgan Freeman
can get a well-earned rest, motherfuckers.

Writer's Block

Waiting months,
crippled by the dusk of my life
for a vision veiled in a raindrop

as it burst across my forehead,
I strained to explain the words a tree spoke
and the song in a storm cloud.

Once, dandelions were more than weeds
and wolves felt more than hunger.
But all that sacred insight escaped me.

What I thought I should feel was not
what I thought I felt, as if the head
might free the heart and not the opposite.

Then, my car roared along Route10
past a battered truck that smoked
and snorted in the lane beside me.

Painted on the truck door in florid green,
a sign read "stump grinding"
and I could think only of Barbara Ann

dancing as she stripped in some crummy bar
not far from the Ohio River.
I was eighteen and drinking beer there

served to me through virtue of my fake I.D.
I fell in love, dizzy with vertigo in the height
of my delusion and the sight of her nipples.

She pleaded softly, “buy me some champagne,”
her body, sad and hypnotic, swayed rhythmically
like the old truck, and there it was, labeled

inspiration by those who never have it and braided
in the sweet smell of wood shavings, diesel fuel,
cheap perfume, and a glass of lukewarm champagne.

Shopping for Allen Ginsberg

(after "A Supermarket in California")

What thoughts I have of you tonight, Allen. I'm on fire, not one of those wildfires that recently ripped across the California freeways, not some smoldering Sulphur mess in an overfull landfill or on the outskirts of hell, not even a suburbanite grill flame charring a steak. This fire is all internal sound and blood. All I'm doing is shopping for produce in a fluorescent aisle of the local Kroger's. What is my problem? The melons have soft spots, the tomatoes overpriced and unripe. The hiss of the mist that waters the browning lettuce startles me. Every banana bruised.

The whole world rots and I can't seem to stop it.

At 3 A.M. a voice whispers from behind the cabbage.
"Where are you going, Jim? Which way does your beard point?"

I wish I could have known Grace Slick when I was younger, when sex was like a handshake—just a way to say hello—and the drugs I took gave me insight before they brought the numbness of knowledge. It was a time when time passed the way sunrise stumbles across the beach, jumping over starfish, puppy-clumsy and playful, sharing light forever, when I hoped that the dream of America was America. If the future did not belong to the past, would I be alone, your poem in my mind, in this supermarket searching for meaning among the avocadoes old mother of the Beats, midwife to my generation?

In a dying America, what happens when we mistake our hunger for a simple lack of food?

Night Chorale in the Desert

In Death Valley voices
ascend from grains of sand
stirred into a chorus by the night wind.
If it sounds more as moan than melody,
then you're not listening well enough
as ancient tribes of the Paiute people did.
Those nomads mimicked loyally
on wooden flutes and leather drums
the steady pulse and balance of our lives
sung by the dark world above the cactus.
Around their fires the music they knew
praised all they did not know.
Some have called this worship, some
might call it blasphemy, and others
scorn it for the childish wailing
of unwashed savages. Perhaps
it's nothing more than wishful thought
from a people thankful for the earth.
As birds unaware of why there was air
flew unafraid into the sky, they shared
untethered and reborn in oneness
the refrain that gave them life.

Unraveling Wallace Stevens on Easter

My death will be a slight mistake made by a small deity.

Some see their own death as an injustice inflicted on them
by the Devil, others as retribution by the only true God.
When a child dies, or a pet cat for the childless, some say
they are needed to populate a better place.

The faithless argue the dead go nowhere. Dying is natural,
like rain falling or a river refilling the sea.

Not being satisfied with any of those accounts, I'd prefer
living forever, especially as one of the idle rich.
My existential aversion to the act of dying, expressly
when used as a verb—to pass over, transition, go belly up,
kick the bucket, screw the pooch, bite the dust, take a dirt nap,
or become fender meat—is well known to all manner of beings
including, and just in case, a large pantheon of immortal creatures.

When I Was Six Years Old

My father took me to the county fair
and there, he bought a round balloon,
red, white, and blue, filled with helium
that made it lighter than the August air.

Tied to my wrist the thing bounced,
twirled, bobbed, and swirled as we
stepped off down the midway past
the taffy stand, the carnie games,
the Ferris wheel, the rocket-planes
the tilt-a-whirl, and the banging
bumper cars in its insane effort
to break free from childish savagery.

In and out of shadows cast
by neon lights and kaleidoscopic
costumes of the barkers at the show tents,
I felt safe by my father's side

and warm in the electric hum of engines
that drove the rides until I could resist
no more the restless call of a dark desire
to test the borders of my restraint and released
the balloon from around my wrist.
Unbound, it drifted upward free to tour
the night sky unfettered and unconcerned
that even unchained it might never reach the stars.

Epilogue:

Taking Flight with Rahsaan Roland Kirk

I listen

To the blue

of Night

blown

across a silver

flute

of moonlight

by the lip

of a bird's wing

Watch

the sky melt

into a velvet river

flowing

like the breath

of a sleeping tiger

www.ingramcontent.com/pod-product-compliance
Lightning Source LLC
Chambersburg PA
CBHW050022170726
48282CB00025B/514
9788182539624